IT'S OK TO BE SENSITIVE IT'S OK TO BE SENSITIVE IT'S OK TO BE SENSITIVE IT'S OK TO BE SENSITIVE IT'S OK TO BE SENSITIVE IT'S OK TO BE SENSITIVE IT'S OK TO BE SENSITIVE IT'S OK TO BE SENSITIVE IT'S OK TO BE SENSITIVE IT'S OK TO BE SENSITIVE IT'S OK TO BE SENSITIVE IT'S OK TO BE SENSITIVE IT'S OK TO BE SENSITIVE IT'S OK TO BE SENSITIVE

This journal belongs to

_____,

a sensitive soul.

Created, published, and distributed by Knock Knock
6080 Center Drive
Los Angeles, CA 90045
knockknockstuff.com
Knock Knock is a registered trademark of
Knock Knock LLC

© 2019 Knock Knock LLC
All rights reserved
Printed in China

No part of this product may be used or reproduced in any manner whatsoever without prior written permission from the publisher, except in the case of brief quotations embodied in critical articles and reviews. For information, address Knock Knock.

Where specific company, product, and brand names are cited, copyright and trademarks associated with these names are property of their respective owners. Every reasonable attempt has been made to identify owners of copyright. Errors or omissions will be corrected in subsequent editions.

ISBN: 978-168349189-7
UPC: 825703-50191-9

10 9 8 7 6 5 4 3 2 1

IT'S OK TO BE SENSITIVE

Today's Note-to-Self: It's OK to be sensitive about…

It's very hard to be vulnerable, but those people who do that are the dreamers, the thinkers and the creators. They are the magic people of the world.

Amy Poehler

Today's Note-to-Self: It's OK to be totally…

People have said "Don't cry" to other people for years and years, and all it has ever meant is "I'm too uncomfortable when you show your feelings: Don't cry." I'd rather have them say, "Go ahead and cry. I'm here to be with you."

Mr. Rogers

Today's Note-to-Self: It's OK to wish that…

Everything hurts. Because we are

soft beings called humans. Yoko Ono

I find it extremely impossible not to cry when I hear Stevie Nicks's "Landslide," especially the lyric: "I've been afraid of changing, because I've built my life around you." I think a good test to see if a human is actually a robot/android/cylon is to have them listen to this song lyric and study their reaction. If they don't cry, you should stab them through the heart. You will find a fusebox.

Mindy Kaling

Today's Note-to-Self: It's OK if people think I'm…

Today's Note-to-Self: It's OK to do things like…

Bring me all of your dreams,
You dreamers,
Bring me all of your
Heart melodies
That I may wrap them
In a blue cloud-cloth
Away from the too-rough fingers
Of the world.

Langston Hughes

Today's Note-to-Self: It's OK to be super excited about…

You know what? I'm weak a lot. I'm a little lost and confused and sensitive and insecure sometimes and that's all right with me because I'm pretty sure that's just what it means to be HUMAN. That's my kind of STRONG. None of this fake bravado, please. Be real. You don't need to be SuperHuman— Just Be human.

Glennon Doyle

Today's Note-to-Self: It's OK to not…

The whole basis of my singing is feeling.

Unless I feel something, I can't sing.   Billie Holiday

> You may be sensitive INSIDE, but what I see on the outside is a SOLDIER.
>
> Lauren Graham

Today's Note-to-Self: It's OK to speak up about…

I feel groggy and weary and tragic,
Punchy and bleary and fresh out of magic
But alive, but alive, but alive!

I feel twitchy and bitchy and manic,
Calm and collected and choking with panic
But alive, but alive, but alive!

Charles Strouse

Today's Note-to-Self: It's OK that my bestie and I…

Today's Note-to-Self: It's OK to treat myself to…

Don't be afraid to feel as angry because when you feel nothing, or as loving as you can, it's just death. Lena Horne

The truly creative mind in any field is no more than this: A human creature born abnormally, inhumanly sensitive. To him ... a touch is a blow, a sound is a noise, a misfortune is a tragedy, a joy is an ecstasy.

Pearl S. Buck

Today's Note-to-Self: It's OK if I start…

Today's Note-to-Self: It's OK to lose…

You cannot protect yourself from yourself from happiness.

sadness without protecting

Jonathan Safran Foer

Today's Note-to-Self: It's OK to be hurt when…

Most people walk into a room and perhaps notice the furniture, the people—that's about it. Highly sensitive people can be instantly aware, whether they wish to be or not, of the mood, the friendships and enmities, the freshness or staleness of the air, the personality of the one who arranged the flowers.

Elaine Aron

Today's Note-to-Self: It's OK to be, like,…

When I grow up I want to be a little boy.

Joseph Heller

We carry accumulation of years in our bodies, and on our faces, but generally our real selves, the children inside, are innocent and shy as magnolias.

Maya Angelou

Today's Note-to-Self: It's OK to go all out and…

Today's Note-to-Self: It's OK to need more…

For my part, I prefer
It is so lovely, dawn-kaleidoscopic

my heart to be broken.
within the crack. D. H. Lawrence

Today's Note-to-Self: It's OK that I'm so…

I cry all the time, I am a crier. I cried last night.

Priyanka Chopra

Today's Note-to-Self: It's OK to high-five myself for…

That's what life is all about.
So you'd better cry now

There's a lot of crying involved. and get used to it. Ellen DeGeneres

Today's Note-to-Self: It's OK to believe…

Anything is possible. Stay open, forever, so open it hurts, and then open up some more, until the day you die, world without end, amen.

George Saunders

Today's Note-to-Self: It's OK for me and you-know-who to…

When we were children, we used to think that when we were grown-up we would no longer be vulnerable. But to grow up is to accept vulnerability.

Madeleine L'Engle

For me, there's no way of life where I'm not completely showing my ass. The artifice of everyone walking around pretending like we know exactly what is going on—there are times when I just can't take it. I just want the world to be softer and more vulnerable.

Heather Havrilesky

Today's Note-to-Self: It's OK if it takes me…

Today's Note-to-Self: It's OK to feel all the feels when…

I think of myself as an intelligent, sensitive
always forces me to blow it at the

human being with the soul of a clown—which
most important moments. Jim Morrison

Today's Note-to-Self: It's OK to vent by…

I was broken and then I broke yet healed but I have started

some more, and I am not believing I will be.   Roxane Gay

Today's Note-to-Self: It's OK to secretly hope…

Sometimes i think
i need a spare
heart to feel
all the things I feel.

Sanober Khan

Today's Note-to-Self: It's OK that I don't always…

It was okay to get scared, and it was okay to get depressed, and it was okay to cry and scream and mourn my health and get it out of my system. I thought I had to be a brave soldier...I always found that after a really good cry, I felt better about everything. I felt as though I got rid of some toxicity, that I got rid of some of the pain and the mourning.

Gilda Radner

Today's Note-to-Self: It's OK to want…

Don't be afraid of suffering. Facing darkness better to go into the suffering and figure being afraid of it. This emotional pain is always really uncomfortable. It's out what it really feels like instead of is what binds us all. Margaret Cho

There's, like, this fight between courage and fear. And sometimes we choose fear because we want to protect ourselves. But we don't realize that by choosing fear, we put ourselves in a situation that has a really bad impact on us.

Malala Yousafzai

Today's Note-to-Self: It's OK when…

Today's Note-to-Self: It's OK to be confused about…

> I do feel that softness for the vulnerability and the innocence in our world, including my own.
>
> Jane Lynch

sometimes I want to hug all
Mankind on earth
and say,
god damn all this that they've
brought down upon us

Charles Bukowski

Today's Note-to-Self: It's OK to be seriously…

Today's Note-to-Self: It's OK to say…

Beauty of whatever kind, in its
excites the sensitive

upreme development, invariably
oul to tears. Edgar Allan Poe

Today's Note-to-Self: It's OK to LOL about…

The memory of things gone is important to a jazz musician. Things like old folks singing in the moonlight in the back yard on a hot night or something said long ago.

Louis Armstrong

Today's Note-to-Self: It's OK to feel iffy about…

You can experience only as much joy as you have had sorrow. Sorrow is like the hollowing out of a wooden block, and joy is what fills it up. The more sorrow you've had, the deeper the joy you can experience.

Dhani Harrison

Today's Note-to-Self: It's OK that it drives me bonkers when…

I don't want to have a thick skin, because if things in either. So, I prefer to be permeable. You know, they can be really upset, they look at them and it's over. And that's

you have a thick skin, you don't let the good
like a child. Have you seen how children are?
can cry, and then five minutes later, you
how I like to be. Arianna Huffington

Today's Note-to-Self: It's OK to wonder…

Your days are numbered. Use them to throw open the windows of your soul to the sun.

Marcus Aurelius

Today's Note-to-Self: It's OK if I stop…

Janie looked down on him and felt a self-crushing love. So her soul crawled out from its hiding place.

Zora Neale Hurston

Today's Note-to-Self: It's OK to show…

When it finally briefly happens, happiness

Today's Note-to-Self: It's OK that I didn't…

Agonies are one of my changes of garments, I do not ask the wounded person how he feels, I myself become the wounded person.

Walt Whitman

It always felt like I was on an operating table and the anesthesia never worked.

RuPaul

Today's Note-to-Self: It's OK that I'm not…

Today's Note-to-Self: It's OK to think it's cool when…

You are already naked. There is no reason

"Real isn't how you are made," said the Skin Horse. "It's a thing that happens to you. When a child loves you for a long, long time, not just to play with, but REALLY loves you, then you become Real."

"Does it hurt?" asked the Rabbit.

"Sometimes," said the Skin Horse, for he was always truthful. "When you are Real you don't mind being hurt."

Margery Williams

Today's Note-to-Self: It's OK because…

Have you ever been in love? Horrible isn't it? It makes you so vulnerable. It opens your chest and it opens up your heart and it means that someone can get inside you and mess you up.

Neil Gaiman

Today's Note-to-Self: It's OK to have a…

I love that I have learned to trust people with

my heart, even if it will get broken.   Johnny Weir

Today's Note-to-Self: It's OK to wanna cry about…

> There is no intensity of love or feeling that does not involve the risk of crippling hurt. It is a duty to take this risk, to love and feel without defense or reserve.
>
> William S. Burroughs

Today's Note-to-Self: It's OK to wear…

Oh, the loneliness in this world
Well it's just not fair
Hey, love and mercy, that's what we need tonight
So love and mercy to you and your friends tonight

Brian Wilson

Today's Note-to-Self: It's OK that I kind of blew it when…

There can be no vulnerability without risk. There
There can be no peace—and ultimately no

Today's Note-to-Self: It's OK blah blah blah...

Those who choose not to empathize enable
an act of outright evil ourselves, we collude

...real monsters. For without ever committing... with it, through our own apathy. J. K. Rowling

I believe empathy is the most essential quality of civilization.

Roger Ebert

Today's Note-to-Self: It's OK to rant about…

Today's Note-to-Self: It's OK if people don't…

Manners are a sensitive awareness of the feelings of others. If you have that awareness, you have good manners, no matter what fork you use.

Emily Post

Today's Note-to-Self: It's OK to love…

My work is delicate; it may
True strength is delicate. My

look strong, but it is delicate.
whole life is in it.   Louise Nevelson

Only people who are capable of loving strongly can also suffer great sorrow, but this same necessity of loving serves to counteract their grief and heals them.

Leo Tolstoy

Today's Note-to-Self: It's OK to hate it when…

I've been looking around and I noticed something: how much you really need to be loved. Ambition isn't just a desperate quest for positions or money. It's just love—lots of love.

Janis Joplin

Today's Note-to-Self: It's OK to say screw it and…

Today's Note-to-Self: It's OK to need less…

I'm trying to figure it out. I'm so confused. What I really learned about love? That it hurts. I'm really super feminine, and I'm really soft. I'm very sensitive, I realized.

Serena Williams

Some people say, "Never let them see you cry." I say, if you're so mad you could just cry, then cry. It terrifies everyone.

Tina Fey

Today's Note-to-Self: It's OK that I haven't got…

Today's Note-to-Self: It's OK that I still…

One day when I was sitting quiet and feeling like a motherless child, which I was, it come to me: that feeling of being part of everything, not separate at all. I knew that if I cut a tree, my arm would bleed. And I laughed and I cried and I run all around the house. I knew just what it was. In fact, when it happen, you can't miss it.

Alice Walker

Today's Note-to-Self: It's OK to freak out because…

I find my emotions are way more accessible than they were when I was younger and I've come to feel it has to do with age… I feel myself becoming part of everything, as if I bleed into other people's joy and pain.

Jane Fonda

People are so aggressive, I can't take all that. I need to go *home*, I need to look at the grass. I'm always writing about my English garden.

John Lennon

Today's Note-to-Self: It's OK even if…

Today's Note-to-Self: It's OK to ask for…

It gives you a good feeling. Each
the magic of life. A flower arrives and it
and it looks fantastic. There is a
can't help but be sensitive

year you rediscover in a garden
is a miracle. The leaves fall in the autumn
tenderness about a garden and you
to that.   Hubert de Givenchy

Anything beautiful is worth getting hurt for.

Prince

Today's Note-to-Self: It's OK to hold on to…

Today's Note-to-Self: It's OK that I couldn't even…

I don't mean to be so sensitive, but that's just who I am. And I'm not afraid to admit it.

Tiffany Haddish

Today's Note-to-Self: It's OK when I miss…

Don't allow the coldness and fear of
beating heart. Nothing is more powerful than
Whether it's a song, a stranger, a mountain,
a footstep, feel it all—look around you

others to tarnish your perfectly vulnerable
allowing yourself to truly be affected by things.
a raindrop, a tea kettle, an article, a sentence,
All of this is for you. Amelia Olson

So sensitive, said a family friend, that she could feel the grass grow under her feet.

Bill Roorbach

Today's Note-to-Self: It's OK to create…

Today's Note-to-Self: It's OK to be pissed about…

What a man does for pay is of little instrument responsive to the world's significance. What he is, as a sensitive beauty, is everything! — H. P. Lovecraft

Today's Note-to-Self: It's OK to feel…

> Whenever I drink Champagne, I either laugh or cry…I get so emotional! I love Champagne.
>
> Tina Turner

Today's Note-to-Self: It's OK to like it when…

Both men and women should feel free to be sensitive. Both men and women should feel free to be strong.

Emma Watson

Today's Note-to-Self: It's OK to think that…

Live on, survive, for the earth gives your heart, but the wonders keep

Sometimes if you expose your vulnerability, someone else will feel comforted. It's like we're all in this boat together.

Tavi Gevinson

Today's Note-to-Self: It's OK to give myself a break because…

Why can't we give love give love give love give love give love
Give love give love give love give love give love give love?
'Cause love's such an old-fashioned word
And love dares you to care for
The people on the edge of the night
And love dares you to change our way of
Caring about ourselves

Queen and David Bowie

Today's Note-to-Self: It's OK to spend too much time…

Today's Note-to-Self: It's OK to get mad when…

> Maybe part of our formal education should be training in empathy. Imagine how different the world would be if, in fact, that were "reading, writing, arithmetic, empathy."
>
> Neil deGrasse Tyson

Today's Note-to-Self: It's OK to let go of…

Open your hands if you

want to be held. Rumi

"I hate you" she said to me one afternoon. "I really, really hate you." Call me sensitive, but I couldn't help but take it personally.

David Sedaris

Today's Note-to-Self: It's OK that I…

Go forth and feel.

IT'S OK TO BE SENSITIVE IT'S OK TO BE SENSITIVE IT'S OK TO BE SENSITIVE IT'S OK TO BE SENSITIVE IT'S OK TO BE SENSITIVE IT'S OK TO BE SENSITIVE IT'S OK TO BE SENSITIVE IT'S OK TO BE SENSITIVE IT'S OK TO BE SENSITIVE IT'S OK TO BE SENSITIVE IT'S OK TO BE SENSITIVE IT'S OK TO BE SENSITIVE IT'S OK TO BE SENSITIVE IT'S OK TO BE SENSITIVE IT'S OK TO BE SENSITIVE IT'S OK TO BE SEN